Putting Down

What You Put Up

Preserver's Journal

DIANE DUNAS

Diane Dunas

Culinary Arts Ltd., Publisher

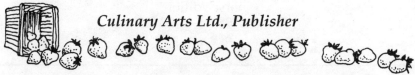

Preserver's Journal: Putting Down What You Put Up
Copyright © 1996 by Diane Dunas

Printed in the United States of America.
ISBN 0-914667-17-3

Cover & Interior Art by Janora Bayot
Graphic Design by PMH Design
Editor: Cheryl Long

Other Books by Culinary Arts Ltd.

Classic Liqueurs: The Art of Making & Cooking With Liqueurs
The Best of Scanfest: A Treasury of Authentic Recipes & Proverbs
Easy Microwave Preserving
Gourmet Mustards: How To Make & Cook With Them
Gourmet Vinegars: How To Make & Cook With Them
Lamb Country Cooking: Lamb With All The Trimmings

Publishers catalog available upon request

Culinary Arts Ltd.
P.O. Box 2157
Lake Oswego, OR. 97035
503-639-4549
503-620-4933 fax

First Edition
96 97 98 99 - 5 4 3 2 1

This Journal contains

the recipes and preserving records of -

_____

_____

"Fired with a housewifely wish to see her
store-room stocked with homemade preserves,
she undertook to put up her currant jelly.
(Meg) spent a long day picking, boiling,
straining, and fussing over her jelly.
She did her best;
she asked advice of Mrs. Cornelius;
she racked her brain to remember what Hannah did
that she had left undone;
she reboiled, resugared, and restrained, but...
The - the jelly won't jell
and I don't know what to do!"

Louisa May Alcott
Little Women, 1892 edition

Canning Time

There's a wondrous smell of spices
In the kitchen,
Most bewitchin';
There are fruits cut into slices
That just set the palate itchin';
There's the sound of spoon on platter
And the rattle and the clatter;
And a bunch of kids are hastin'
To the splendid joy of tastin';
It's the fragrant time of year
When fruit-cannin' days are here.

There's a good wife gayly smilin'
And perspirin'
Some, and tirin';
And while jar on jar she's pilin'
And the necks o' them she's wirin'
I'm a-sittin' here an' dreamin'
Of the kettles that are steamin',
And the cares that have been troublin'
All have vanished in the bubblin'.
I am happy that I'm here
At the cannin' time of year.

Lord, I'm sorry for the feller
That is missin'
All the hissin'
Of the juices, red and yeller
And can never sit and listen
To the rattle and the clatter
Of the sound of spoon on platter.
I am sorry for the single,
For they miss the thrill and tingle
Of the splendid time of year
When the cannin' days are here.

Edgar A. Guest, 1916

Contents

Acknowledgements

*7*hank you to Nellie Oehler and the Master Food Preservers of Lane County Extension Service, Eugene, Oregon for providing so much information and wonderful hints. And to my parents, my husband and our three children; Theresa, Elizabeth and Stanley, for encouraging me to write this journal and preserve foods.

To memories of my Grandma Ray, who in her later years would sit by the stove in her wheelchair stirring her rhubarb. Breakfast, lunch or dinner was always the right time to eat her special rhubarb. She wasn't able to have a garden, but she always had a rhubarb plant in her yard which yielded enough to make many jars of rhubarb for her pantry. She reminded me that we can all enjoy and take satisfaction in preserving, however limited it might be.

Come ye thankful people
Come raise the song of Harvest-home:
All is safely gathered in
Ere the winter storms begin.

Henry Alford, 1810-1871

*A*fter a busy summer of gardening, preserving and trying to keep track of all my efforts, I thought, "There has to be a better way!" I had been scribbling notes year after year in the back of cookbooks regarding the recipes I used for spaghetti sauce, or just how much sugar was perfect in the syrup for pears and peaches, etc. Out of my frustration came the ideas and organization for the *Preserver's Journal*.

The *Preserver's Journal* is for all who have a heart for homemade, healthy and special recipes all year long. It is also for those who simply make a batch or two of your eagerly requested chutney or jam for holiday or celebration gifts. I have included gift giving pages just for this purpose. I find homemade gifts from my kitchen so welcome and unique!

The ultimate purpose of this journal is to record your recipes as only you know them, to note the amount preserved each year and to record comments and reminders. The Journal is meant to last even the busiest preserver for years and then to serve as reference and eventually an heirloom family recipe record.

You will save time, money and the frustration of trying to find that special recipe or note when it's time to preserve again. My Yield Conversions, Local Harvest Time, Helpful Hot Line Phone Numbers, and other essential preservation information are all designed to put everything you need for an efficient, enjoyable preserving season at your fingertips.

My wish is that you use this journal as a tool to make preserving foods the satisfying and rewarding experience it is meant to be. Write down all of your hints, secrets and special notes for each item preserved. Year after year your journal notes will be handy and one day become a treasured family keepsake.

Diane Dunas
Master Food Preserver

Local Harvest Time

To assist your preservation planning put a check mark for the month that a particular fruit or vegetable is ready for harvest in your area. Use the blank spaces at the bottom of the page for produce not on the list.

JAN-FEB-MAR-APR-MAY-JUN-JUL-AUG-SEP-OCT-NOV-DEC

Apples _____
Apricots _____
Artichokes _____
Asparagus _____
Beans _____
Beets _____
Blackberries _____
Blueberries _____
Broccoli _____
Brussel
* Sprouts* _____
Cabbage _____
Carrots _____
Cauliflower _____
Cherries _____
Corn _____
Cranberries _____
Grapes _____
Nectarines _____
Onions _____
Peaches _____
Pears _____
Peas _____
Peppers _____
Plums _____
Potatoes _____
Pumpkins _____
Raspberries _____
Rhubarb _____
Spinach _____
Squash _____
Strawberries _____
Tomatoes _____
Zucchini _____

_____
_____
_____
_____

Equivalent Measures

1 pinch = less than 1/8 teaspoon (dry)
1 dash = 3 drops to 1/4 teaspoon (liquid)
1 teaspoon = 4.9 milliliters
3 teaspoons = 1 tablespoon = 1/2 ounce = 14 grams
2 tablespoons =1 ounce = 28 grams
4 tablespoons = 2 ounces = 1/4 cup = 55 grams
5 1/3 tablespoons = 1/3 cup
16 tablespoons = 1 cup = 8 ounces = 1/2 pound = 228 grams
2 cups =1 pint = 1 pound = 454 grams
2 pints = 1 quart = 2 pounds = 908 grams
4 quarts (liquid) = 1 gallon = 8 pounds

Formula for Metric Conversion

Cups to liters	multiply cups by .24
Ounces to grams	multiply ounces by 28.35
Grams to ounces	multiply grams by .035
Pounds to grams	multiply pounds by 453.5
Pounds to kilograms	multiply pounds by .45

Equivalents

1 pound apples = 3 medium apples
3 pounds apples = 8 cups pared, sliced apples
2 large bananas = 1 pound = 1 1/2 cups
1 3/4 - 2 cups berries = 1 pint berries
8 ounces pitted dates = 1 1/4 cups chopped dates
1 tablespoon fresh herbs = 1 teaspoon dried herbs
Juice of 1 lemon = 2 - 3 tablespoons lemon juice
Juice of 1 orange = 1/4 - 1/3 cup orange juice
1 medium onion = 1/2 cup chopped onion
1 pound brown sugar = 2 1/4 cups firmly packed brown sugar
1 pound granulated sugar = 2 1/4 cups granulated sugar

Emergency Substitutions

Ingredient	Substitute
1 cup granulated sugar	7/8 cup honey
1 cup granulated sugar	1 cup maple syrup plus 1/4 cup corn syrup
1 cup granulated sugar	1 cup molasses plus 1 teaspoon baking soda
1 cup light corn syrup	1 1/4 cup sugar plus 1/3 cup liquid
1 cup honey	1 1/4 cup sugar plus 1/4 cup liquid
caster sugar	superfine granulated sugar, equal measure
treacle	molasses (any variety)
1 cup whole milk	1/2 cup evaporated milk plus 1/2 cup water or 1 cup reconstituted nonfat dry milk plus 2 tablespoons butter/margarine

HINTS FOR USING YOUR
Items Preserved Pages

ITEM PRESERVED

The *Item Preserved* pages are the heart of your journal. Label your item preserved at the top of the page. (I show my example of this and the other parts of the record in the sample following.)

RECIPE OR METHOD USED

This is your opportunity to write your "own" recipe down, which you or your family may have perfected over the years. Remember to also record the method of preserving you used and any special notes for next year.

RUNNING TALLY

Use the *Running Tally* to record the amount of pints, quarts, etc. preserved as you go, to eliminate counting at the end. This is especially helpful when your preserving takes up to a week or more for an item and everything is put away by the time you want to count it.

MONTH & YEAR ITEM PRESERVED

Basic information that is very handy for reference.

AMOUNT PUT UP

The *Amount Put Up* is the total of your running tally. Be sure and label your quantity as to pints, quarts, etc. too.

AMOUNT LEFT OVER OR DATE RAN OUT

This lets you record how your supply lasted to the next season. For instance, did you end up 20 quarts short, or did you have 15 pints too much?

COMMENTS

This lets you keep track of how the recipe was received. For example, you may have found the applesauce had too much cinnamon for the family.

NOTES FOR NEXT YEAR

This is a catch-all for your notes. The things you want to be *sure* and remember next year! It's a good place to note how much to preserve next year or quanity to plant in your garden.

"If you can organize your kitchen you can organize your life."
Louis Parrish

Item preserved: _Elberta Peaches_

Recipe or method used: _Dip peaches in boiling water to loosen skins. Next dip into cold water and remove skins. Cut into halves. Raw pack into wide mouthed jars, pour medium syrup (3¼ cups sugar with 5 cups water) over peaches. Process in water bath for 25 minutes for pint jars and 30 minutes for quarts._

Month & Year item preserved: _July, 1995_

Running tally: _₦₦ ₦₦ ₦₦ ₦₦ ₦₦_

Amount put up: _28 quarts_

Amount left over, or date ran out: _Ran out on Mar/'96_

Comments: _Peaches had a nice texture and color. Family thought a little on the sweet side._

Notes for next year: _Stick with the Improved Elbertas. Preserve more quarts. Use a light syrup recipe — (2¼ cups sugar with 5¼ cups water)._

13

Item Preserved: Apricot Pineapple Jam

Recipe or method used: _____

In 8 qt. pot mix

　　3C diced apricots (2 pds.)

　　20 oz crushed or diced pineapple chunks
　　　　　　　　　　　　　(undrained)

　　½ C lemon juice

　　Stir in 1 Box (mc) pectin & ½ tsp. butter

Bring to full rolling boil

Stir in 8C sugar

Bring to boil for 4 minutes

Skim foam

Can

Month & Year item preserved: _____

Running tally: _____

Amount put up: _____

Amount left over, or date ran out: _____

Comments: _____

Notes for next year: _____

Use a wax pencil or crayon to label information on hot lids.

Month &Year item preserved: _____

Running tally: _____

Amount put up: _____

Amount left over, or date ran out: _____

Comments: _____

_____

_____

Notes for next year: _____

Month &Year item preserved: _____

Running tally: _____

Amount put up: _____

Amount left over, or date ran out: _____

Comments: _____

_____

_____

Notes for next year: _____

Month &Year item preserved: _____

Running tally: _____

Amount put up: _____

Amount left over, or date ran out: _____

Comments: _____

_____

_____

Notes for next year: _____

Month &Year item preserved: _____

Running tally: _____

Amount put up: _____

Amount left over, or date ran out: _____

Comments: _____

_____

_____

Notes for next year: _____

Item Preserved: _Fresh Blackberry Vinegar_

Recipe or method used: _____

_____

_____

_____

_____

_____

_____

_____

_____

_____

_____

_____

_____

_____

_____

_____

_____

_____

_____

_____

_____

_____

_____

Month & Year item preserved: _____

Running tally: _____

Amount put up: _____

Amount left over, or date ran out: _____

Comments: _From "Sweet Home Alabama" Cook book_

Notes for next year: _____

"Marmalade in the morning has the same effect on the taste buds
that a cold shower has on the body." Jeanine Larmoth

Month &Year item preserved: _____

Running tally: _____

Amount put up: _____

Amount left over, or date ran out: _____

Comments: _____

_____

_____

Notes for next year: _____

Month &Year item preserved: _____

Running tally: _____

Amount put up: _____

Amount left over, or date ran out: _____

Comments: _____

_____

_____

Notes for next year: _____

Month &Year item preserved: _____

Running tally: _____

Amount put up: _____

Amount left over, or date ran out: _____

Comments: _____

_____

_____

Notes for next year: _____

Month &Year item preserved: _____

Running tally: _____

Amount put up: _____

Amount left over, or date ran out: _____

Comments: _____

_____

_____

Notes for next year: _____

Item Preserved: _____

Recipe or method used: _____

_____

_____

_____

_____

_____

_____

_____

_____

_____

_____

_____

_____

_____

_____

_____

_____

_____

_____

_____

_____

Month & Year item preserved: _____

Running tally: _____

Amount put up: _____

Amount left over, or date ran out: _____

Comments: _____

_____

Notes for next year: _____

*Preserve basil leaves by pureeing them with a little oil,
freeze and use all year round.*

Month & Year item preserved: _____

Running tally: _____

Amount put up: _____

Amount left over, or date ran out: _____

Comments: _____

_____

_____

Notes for next year: _____

Month & Year item preserved: _____

Running tally: _____

Amount put up: _____

Amount left over, or date ran out: _____

Comments: _____

_____

_____

Notes for next year: _____

Month & Year item preserved: _____

Running tally: _____

Amount put up: _____

Amount left over, or date ran out: _____

Comments: _____

_____

_____

Notes for next year: _____

Month & Year item preserved: _____

Running tally: _____

Amount put up: _____

Amount left over, or date ran out: _____

Comments: _____

_____

_____

Notes for next year: _____

Item Preserved: _____

Recipe or method used: _____

_____

_____

_____

_____

_____

_____

_____

_____

_____

_____

_____

_____

_____

_____

_____

_____

_____

_____

_____

_____

_____

_____

_____

_____

Month &Year item preserved: _____

Running tally: _____

Amount put up: _____

Amount left over, or date ran out: _____

Comments: _____

_____

_____

Notes for next year: _____

Many people ask, "Can one make liquid pectin from dry pectin?"
The answer is no, because dry pectin is made from citrus products,
while the liquid pectin is from apples.

Month & Year item preserved: _____

Running tally: _____

Amount put up: _____

Amount left over, or date ran out: _____

Comments: _____

_____

_____

Notes for next year: _____

_____

Month & Year item preserved: _____

Running tally: _____

Amount put up: _____

Amount left over, or date ran out: _____

Comments: _____

_____

_____

Notes for next year: _____

_____

Month & Year item preserved: _____

Running tally: _____

Amount put up: _____

Amount left over, or date ran out: _____

Comments: _____

_____

_____

Notes for next year: _____

_____

Month & Year item preserved: _____

Running tally: _____

Amount put up: _____

Amount left over, or date ran out: _____

Comments: _____

_____

_____

Notes for next year: _____

_____

Item Preserved: _____

Recipe or method used: _____

_____

_____

_____

_____

_____

_____

_____

_____

_____

_____

_____

_____

_____

_____

_____

_____

_____

_____

_____

_____

Month & Year item preserved: _____

Running tally: _____

Amount put up: _____

Amount left over, or date ran out: _____

Comments: _____

_____

Notes for next year: _____

*To prevent fruit from browning while preparing for preservation,
place in a solution of: 1 teaspoon powdered ascorbic acid
or 6 (500 mg.) tablets of Vitamin C per gallon of water.*

Month & Year item preserved: _____

Running tally: _____

Amount put up: _____

Amount left over, or date ran out: _____

Comments: _____

_____

_____

Notes for next year: _____

Month & Year item preserved: _____

Running tally: _____

Amount put up: _____

Amount left over, or date ran out: _____

Comments: _____

_____

_____

Notes for next year: _____

Month & Year item preserved: _____

Running tally: _____

Amount put up: _____

Amount left over, or date ran out: _____

Comments: _____

_____

_____

Notes for next year: _____

Month & Year item preserved: _____

Running tally: _____

Amount put up: _____

Amount left over, or date ran out: _____

Comments: _____

_____

_____

Notes for next year: _____

Item Preserved: _____

Recipe or method used: _____

_____
_____
_____
_____
_____
_____
_____
_____
_____
_____
_____
_____
_____
_____
_____
_____
_____
_____
_____
_____
_____

Month & Year item preserved: _____
Running tally: _____
Amount put up: _____
Amount left over, or date ran out: _____
Comments: _____
_____
_____

Notes for next year: _____

"What was paradise, but a garden full of vegetables and herbs and pleasure? Nothing there but delights." William Lawson

Month & Year item preserved: _____

Running tally: _____

Amount put up: _____

Amount left over, or date ran out: _____

Comments: _____

_____

_____

Notes for next year: _____

_____

Month & Year item preserved: _____

Running tally: _____

Amount put up: _____

Amount left over, or date ran out: _____

Comments: _____

_____

_____

Notes for next year: _____

_____

Month & Year item preserved: _____

Running tally: _____

Amount put up: _____

Amount left over, or date ran out: _____

Comments: _____

_____

_____

Notes for next year: _____

_____

Month & Year item preserved: _____

Running tally: _____

Amount put up: _____

Amount left over, or date ran out: _____

Comments: _____

_____

_____

Notes for next year: _____

_____

Item Preserved: _____

Recipe or method used: _____

_____
_____
_____
_____
_____
_____
_____
_____
_____
_____
_____
_____
_____
_____
_____
_____
_____
_____
_____
_____
_____

Month & Year item preserved: _____
Running tally: _____
Amount put up: _____
Amount left over, or date ran out: _____
Comments: _____
_____
_____

Notes for next year: _____

Dry seedless grapes for wonderful raisins.
Freeze what you're not using.

Month & Year item preserved: _____

Running tally: _____

Amount put up: _____

Amount left over, or date ran out: _____

Comments: _____

_____

_____

Notes for next year: _____

_____

Month & Year item preserved: _____

Running tally: _____

Amount put up: _____

Amount left over, or date ran out: _____

Comments: _____

_____

_____

Notes for next year: _____

_____

Month & Year item preserved: _____

Running tally: _____

Amount put up: _____

Amount left over, or date ran out: _____

Comments: _____

_____

_____

Notes for next year: _____

_____

Month & Year item preserved: _____

Running tally: _____

Amount put up: _____

Amount left over, or date ran out: _____

Comments: _____

_____

_____

Notes for next year: _____

Item Preserved: _____

Recipe or method used: _____

_____

_____

_____

_____

_____

_____

_____

_____

_____

_____

_____

_____

_____

_____

_____

_____

_____

_____

_____

_____

Month & Year item preserved: _____

Running tally: _____

Amount put up: _____

Amount left over, or date ran out: _____

Comments: _____

_____

Notes for next year: _____

*Try strawberry yogurt leather: blend strawberries
(if frozen they should be drained), add yogurt, then dry as usual.*

Month & Year item preserved: _____

Running tally: _____

Amount put up: _____

Amount left over, or date ran out: _____

Comments: _____

_____

_____

Notes for next year: _____

_____

Month & Year item preserved: _____

Running tally: _____

Amount put up: _____

Amount left over, or date ran out: _____

Comments: _____

_____

_____

Notes for next year: _____

_____

Month & Year item preserved: _____

Running tally: _____

Amount put up: _____

Amount left over, or date ran out: _____

Comments: _____

_____

_____

Notes for next year: _____

_____

Month & Year item preserved: _____

Running tally: _____

Amount put up: _____

Amount left over, or date ran out: _____

Comments: _____

_____

_____

Notes for next year: _____

_____

Item Preserved: _____

Recipe or method used: _____

_____

_____

_____

_____

_____

_____

_____

_____

_____

_____

_____

_____

_____

_____

_____

_____

_____

_____

_____

_____

_____

_____

_____

Month & Year item preserved: _____

Running tally: _____

Amount put up: _____

Amount left over, or date ran out: _____

Comments: _____

_____

_____

Notes for next year: _____

Scale or hard water film on canning jars are easily removed
by soaking then in water with some vinegar added.

Month &Year item preserved: _____

Running tally: _____

Amount put up: _____

Amount left over, or date ran out: _____

Comments: _____

_____

_____

Notes for next year: _____

Month &Year item preserved: _____

Running tally: _____

Amount put up: _____

Amount left over, or date ran out: _____

Comments: _____

_____

_____

Notes for next year: _____

Month &Year item preserved: _____

Running tally: _____

Amount Put Up: _____

Amount left over, or date ran out: _____

Comments: _____

_____

_____

Notes for next year: _____

Month &Year item preserved: _____

Running tally: _____

Amount put up: _____

Amount left over, or date ran out: _____

Comments: _____

_____

_____

Notes for next year: _____

Item Preserved: _____

Recipe or method used: _____

_____

_____

_____

_____

_____

_____

_____

_____

_____

_____

_____

_____

_____

_____

_____

_____

_____

_____

_____

_____

_____

Month & Year item preserved: _____

Running tally: _____

Amount put up: _____

Amount left over, or date ran out: _____

Comments: _____

_____

Notes for next year: _____

"In the childhood memories of every good cook, there's a large kitchen, a warm stove, a simmering pot and a mom." Barbara Costikyan

Month & Year item preserved: _____

Running tally: _____

Amount put up: _____

Amount left over, or date ran out: _____

Comments: _____

_____

_____

Notes for next year: _____

Month & Year item preserved: _____

Running tally: _____

Amount put up: _____

Amount left over, or date ran out: _____

Comments: _____

_____

_____

Notes for next year: _____

Month & Year item preserved: _____

Running tally: _____

Amount put up: _____

Amount left over, or date ran out: _____

Comments: _____

_____

_____

Notes for next year: _____

Month & Year item preserved: _____

Running tally: _____

Amount put up: _____

Amount left over, or date ran out: _____

Comments: _____

_____

_____

Notes for next year: _____

Item Preserved: _____

Recipe or method used: _____

_____

_____

_____

_____

_____

_____

_____

_____

_____

_____

_____

_____

_____

_____

_____

_____

_____

_____

_____

_____

_____

Month &Year item preserved: _____

Running tally: _____

Amount put up: _____

Amount left over, or date ran out: _____

Comments: _____

_____

Notes for next year: _____

_____

"When love and skill work together, expect a masterpiece."
John Ruskin

Month & Year item preserved: _____

Running tally: _____

Amount put up: _____

Amount left over, or date ran out: _____

Comments: _____

_____

_____

Notes for next year: _____

Month & Year item preserved: _____

Running tally: _____

Amount put up: _____

Amount left over, or date ran out: _____

Comments: _____

_____

_____

Notes for next year: _____

Month & Year item preserved: _____

Running tally: _____

Amount put up: _____

Amount left over, or date ran out: _____

Comments: _____

_____

_____

Notes for next year: _____

Month & Year item preserved: _____

Running tally: _____

Amount put up: _____

Amount left over, or date ran out: _____

Comments: _____

_____

_____

Notes for next year: _____

Item Preserved: _____

Recipe or method used: _____

_____

_____

_____

_____

_____

_____

_____

_____

_____

_____

_____

_____

_____

_____

_____

_____

_____

_____

_____

_____

_____

Month & Year item preserved: _____

Running tally: _____

Amount put up: _____

Amount left over, or date ran out: _____

Comments: _____

_____

_____

Notes for next year:

_____

For wonderful lunch meat, smoke a whole turkey, slice it and freeze.

Month &Year item preserved: _____

Running tally: _____

Amount put up: _____

Amount left over, or date ran out: _____

Comments: _____

_____

_____

Notes for next year: _____

_____

Month &Year item preserved: _____

Running tally: _____

Amount put up: _____

Amount left over, or date ran out: _____

Comments: _____

_____

_____

Notes for next year: _____

_____

Month &Year item preserved: _____

Running tally: _____

Amount put up: _____

Amount left over, or date ran out: _____

Comments: _____

_____

_____

Notes for next year: _____

_____

Month &Year item preserved: _____

Running tally: _____

Amount put up: _____

Amount left over, or date ran out: _____

Comments: _____

_____

_____

Notes for next year: _____

_____

Item Preserved: _____

Recipe or method used: _____

_____

_____

_____

_____

_____

_____

_____

_____

_____

_____

_____

_____

_____

_____

_____

_____

_____

_____

_____

_____

Month & Year item preserved: _____

Running tally: _____

Amount put up: _____

Amount left over, or date ran out: _____

Comments: _____

_____

_____

Notes for next year: _____

_____

To hot pack pears, apricots, nectarines and peaches, put halves in a frying pan with a sugar syrup and cook until heated through, then pack in jars.

Month & Year item preserved: _____

Running tally: _____

Amount put up: _____

Amount left over, or date ran out: _____

Comments: _____

_____

_____

Notes for next year: _____

_____

Month & Year item preserved: _____

Running tally: _____

Amount put up: _____

Amount left over, or date ran out: _____

Comments: _____

_____

_____

Notes for next year: _____

_____

Month & Year item preserved: _____

Running tally: _____

Amount put up: _____

Amount left over, or date ran out: _____

Comments: _____

_____

_____

Notes for next year: _____

_____

Month & Year item preserved: _____

Running tally: _____

Amount put up: _____

Amount left over, or date ran out: _____

Comments: _____

_____

_____

Notes for next year: _____

_____

Item Preserved: _____

Recipe or method used: _____

_____

_____

_____

_____

_____

_____

_____

_____

_____

_____

_____

_____

_____

_____

_____

_____

_____

_____

_____

_____

Month &Year item preserved: _____

Running tally: _____

Amount put up: _____

Amount left over, or date ran out: _____

Comments: _____

_____

_____

Notes for next year: _____

"For God, who gives seed to the farmer to plant, and later, good crops to harvest and eat, will give you more and more seed to plant and will make it grow so that you can give away more fruit from your harvest." 2 Cor. 9:10

Month &Year item preserved: _____

Running tally: _____

Amount put up: _____

Amount left over, or date ran out: _____

Comments: _____

_____

_____

Notes for next year: _____

Month &Year item preserved: _____

Running tally: _____

Amount put up: _____

Amount left over, or date ran out: _____

Comments: _____

_____

_____

Notes for next year: _____

Month &Year item preserved: _____

Running tally: _____

Amount put up: _____

Amount left over, or date ran out: _____

Comments: _____

_____

_____

Notes for next year: _____

Month &Year item preserved: _____

Running tally: _____

Amount put up: _____

Amount left over, or date ran out: _____

Comments: _____

_____

_____

Notes for next year: _____

Item Preserved: _____

Recipe or method used: _____

_____

_____

_____

_____

_____

_____

_____

_____

_____

_____

_____

_____

_____

_____

_____

_____

_____

_____

_____

_____

_____

Month &Year item preserved: _____

Running tally: _____

Amount put up: _____

Amount left over, or date ran out: _____

Comments: _____

_____

_____

Notes for next year: _____

Before drying apricots, put halves in a frying pan with a sugar syrup and cook until heated through; then dry. Adds a nice color and sweet taste.

Month &Year item preserved: _____

Running tally: _____

Amount put up: _____

Amount left over, or date ran out: _____

Comments: _____

_____

_____

Notes for next year: _____

_____

Month &Year item preserved: _____

Running tally: _____

Amount put up: _____

Amount left over, or date ran out: _____

Comments: _____

_____

_____

Notes for next year: _____

_____

Month &Year item preserved: _____

Running tally: _____

Amount put up: _____

Amount left over, or date ran out: _____

Comments: _____

_____

_____

Notes for next year: _____

_____

Month &Year item preserved: _____

Running tally: _____

Amount put up: _____

Amount left over, or date ran out: _____

Comments: _____

_____

_____

Notes for next year: _____

_____

Item Preserved: _____

Recipe or method used: _____

_____

_____

_____

_____

_____

_____

_____

_____

_____

_____

_____

_____

_____

_____

_____

_____

_____

_____

_____

Month &Year item preserved: _____

Running tally: _____

Amount put up: _____

Amount left over, or date ran out: _____

Comments: _____

_____

_____

Notes for next year: _____

_____

When thawing frozen berries, use the excess juice to make berry syrup.

Month & Year item preserved: _____

Running tally: _____

Amount put up: _____

Amount left over, or date ran out: _____

Comments: _____

_____

_____

Notes for next year: _____

Month & Year item preserved: _____

Running tally: _____

Amount put up: _____

Amount left over, or date ran out: _____

Comments: _____

_____

_____

Notes for next year: _____

Month & Year item preserved: _____

Running tally: _____

Amount put up: _____

Amount left over, or date ran out: _____

Comments: _____

_____

_____

Notes for next year: _____

Month & Year item preserved: _____

Running tally: _____

Amount put up: _____

Amount left over, or date ran out: _____

Comments: _____

_____

_____

Notes for next year: _____

Item Preserved: _____

Recipe or method used: _____

_____

_____

_____

_____

_____

_____

_____

_____

_____

_____

_____

_____

_____

_____

_____

_____

_____

_____

_____

Month & Year item preserved: _____
Running tally: _____
Amount put up: _____
Amount left over, or date ran out: _____
Comments: _____
_____
_____

Notes for next year: _____
_____

*Use berry syrups for pancakes, on top of oatmeal
or with seltzer for an Italian soda.*

Month &Year item preserved: _____

Running tally: _____

Amount put up: _____

Amount left over, or date ran out: _____

Comments: _____

_____

_____

Notes for next year: _____

Month &Year item preserved: _____

Running tally: _____

Amount put up: _____

Amount left over, or date ran out: _____

Comments: _____

_____

_____

Notes for next year: _____

Month &Year item preserved:_____

Running tally: _____

Amount put up: _____

Amount left over, or date ran out: _____

Comments:_____

_____

_____

Notes for next year: _____

Month &Year item preserved: _____

Running tally: _____

Amount put up: _____

Amount left over, or date ran out: _____

Comments: _____

_____

_____

Notes for next year:_____

_____

Item Preserved: _____

Recipe or method used: _____

_____

_____

_____

_____

_____

_____

_____

_____

_____

_____

_____

_____

_____

_____

_____

_____

_____

_____

_____

Month & Year item preserved: _____

Running tally: _____

Amount put up: _____

Amount left over, or date ran out: _____

Comments: _____

_____

Notes for next year: _____

_____

"Tis an ill cook that cannot lick his own fingers."
William Shakespeare

Month &Year item preserved: _____

Running tally: _____

Amount put up: _____

Amount left over, or date ran out: _____

Comments: _____

_____

_____

Notes for next year: _____

_____

Month &Year item preserved: _____

Running tally: _____

Amount put up: _____

Amount left over, or date ran out: _____

Comments: _____

_____

_____

Notes for next year: _____

_____

Month &Year item preserved: _____

Running tally: _____

Amount put up: _____

Amount left over, or date ran out: _____

Comments: _____

_____

_____

Notes for next year: _____

_____

Month &Year item preserved: _____

Running tally: _____

Amount put up: _____

Amount left over, or date ran out: _____

Comments: _____

_____

_____

Notes for next year: _____

_____

Item Preserved: _____

Recipe or method used: _____

_____
_____
_____
_____
_____
_____
_____
_____
_____
_____
_____
_____
_____
_____
_____
_____
_____
_____
_____
_____
_____
_____
_____
_____
_____

Month &Year item preserved: _____
Running tally: _____
Amount put up: _____
Amount left over, or date ran out: _____
Comments: _____
_____
_____

Notes for next year: _____

*Use cornstarch in your spaghetti sauce,
it will adhere to pasta more effectively.*

Month &Year item preserved: _____

Running tally: _____

Amount put up: _____

Amount left over, or date ran out: _____

Comments: _____

_____

_____

Notes for next year: _____

_____

Month &Year item preserved: _____

Running tally: _____

Amount put up: _____

Amount left over, or date ran out: _____

Comments: _____

_____

_____

Notes for next year: _____

_____

Month &Year item preserved: _____

Running tally: _____

Amount put up: _____

Amount left over, or date ran out: _____

Comments: _____

_____

_____

Notes for next year: _____

_____

Month &Year item preserved: _____

Running tally: _____

Amount put up: _____

Amount left over, or date ran out: _____

Comments: _____

_____

_____

Notes for next year: _____

_____

Item Preserved: _____

Recipe or method used: _____

_____
_____
_____
_____
_____
_____
_____
_____
_____
_____
_____
_____
_____
_____
_____
_____
_____
_____
_____
_____
_____
_____
_____
_____
_____

Month & Year item preserved: _____
Running tally: _____
Amount put up: _____
Amount left over, or date ran out: _____
Comments: _____
_____
_____

Notes for next year: _____

For problems, causes, prevention of and other information regarding canning contact your Extension office. They have extensive information on fruits, vegetables, meats, poultry, fish, pickles, relishes, jams and jellies.

Month &Year item preserved: _____

Running tally: _____

Amount put up: _____

Amount left over, or date ran out: _____

Comments: _____

_____

_____

Notes for next year: _____

_____

Month &Year item preserved: _____

Running tally: _____

Amount put up: _____

Amount left over, or date ran out: _____

Comments: _____

_____

_____

Notes for next year: _____

_____

Month &Year item preserved: _____

Running tally: _____

Amount put up: _____

Amount left over, or date ran out: _____

Comments: _____

_____

_____

Notes for next year: _____

_____

Month &Year item preserved: _____

Running tally: _____

Amount put up: _____

Amount left over, or date ran out: _____

Comments: _____

_____

_____

Notes for next year: _____

_____

Item Preserved: _____

Recipe or method used: _____

_____

_____

_____

_____

_____

_____

_____

_____

_____

_____

_____

_____

_____

_____

_____

_____

_____

_____

_____

_____

_____

_____

Month & Year item preserved: _____

Running tally: _____

Amount put up: _____

Amount left over, or date ran out: _____

Comments: _____

_____

_____

Notes for next year: _____

_____

When drying bananas, slice lengthwise or diagonally for a different look.

Month & Year item preserved: _____

Running tally: _____

Amount put up: _____

Amount left over, or date ran out: _____

Comments: _____

_____

_____

Notes for next year: _____

_____

Month & Year item preserved: _____

Running tally: _____

Amount put up: _____

Amount left over, or date ran out: _____

Comments: _____

_____

_____

Notes for next year: _____

_____

Month & Year item preserved: _____

Running tally: _____

Amount put up: _____

Amount left over, or date ran out: _____

Comments: _____

_____

_____

Notes for next year: _____

_____

Month & Year item preserved: _____

Running tally: _____

Amount put up: _____

Amount left over, or date ran out: _____

Comments: _____

_____

_____

Notes for next year: _____

_____

Item Preserved: _____

Recipe or method used: _____

_____

_____

_____

_____

_____

_____

_____

_____

_____

_____

_____

_____

_____

_____

_____

_____

_____

_____

_____

_____

_____

_____

_____

Month & Year item preserved: _____

Running tally: _____

Amount put up: _____

Amount left over, or date ran out: _____

Comments: _____

_____

Notes for next year: _____

_____

"Success is more attitude than aptitude."
Unknown

Month &Year item preserved: _____

Running tally: _____

Amount put up: _____

Amount left over, or date ran out: _____

Comments: _____

_____

_____

Notes for next year: _____

_____

Month &Year item preserved: _____

Running tally: _____

Amount put up: _____

Amount left over, or date ran out: _____

Comments: _____

_____

_____

Notes for next year: _____

_____

Month &Year item preserved: _____

Running tally: _____

Amount put up: _____

Amount left over, or date ran out: _____

Comments: _____

_____

_____

Notes for next year: _____

_____

Month &Year item preserved: _____

Running tally: _____

Amount put up: _____

Amount left over, or date ran out: _____

Comments: _____

_____

_____

Notes for next year: _____

_____

Item Preserved: _____

Recipe or method used: _____

_____

_____

_____

_____

_____

_____

_____

_____

_____

_____

_____

_____

_____

_____

_____

_____

_____

_____

_____

_____

_____

Month & Year item preserved: _____

Running tally: _____

Amount put up: _____

Amount left over, or date ran out: _____

Comments: _____

_____

_____

Notes for next year: _____

_____

*Roll sliced bananas in dry flavored gelatin
then dehydrate for a sweet snack.*

Month &Year item preserved: _____

Running tally: _____

Amount put up: _____

Amount left over, or date ran out: _____

Comments: _____

_____

_____

Notes for next year: _____

Month &Year item preserved: _____

Running tally: _____

Amount put up: _____

Amount left over, or date ran out: _____

Comments: _____

_____

_____

Notes for next year: _____

Month &Year item preserved: _____

Running tally: _____

Amount put up: _____

Amount left over, or date ran out: _____

Comments: _____

_____

_____

Notes for next year: _____

Month &Year item preserved: _____

Running tally: _____

Amount put up: _____

Amount left over, or date ran out: _____

Comments: _____

_____

_____

Notes for next year: _____

Item Preserved: _____

Recipe or method used: _____

_____

_____

_____

_____

_____

_____

_____

_____

_____

_____

_____

_____

_____

_____

_____

_____

_____

_____

_____

_____

Month & Year item preserved: _____

Running tally: _____

Amount put up: _____

Amount left over, or date ran out: _____

Comments: _____

_____

_____

Notes for next year: _____

To organize food in your chest freezer,
place in labeled double paper bags.

Month & Year item preserved: _____

Running tally: _____

Amount put up: _____

Amount left over, or date ran out: _____

Comments: _____

_____

_____

Notes for next year: _____

Month & Year item preserved: _____

Running tally: _____

Amount put up: _____

Amount left over, or date ran out: _____

Comments: _____

_____

_____

Notes for next year: _____

Month & Year item preserved: _____

Running tally: _____

Amount put up: _____

Amount left over, or date ran out: _____

Comments: _____

_____

_____

Notes for next year: _____

Month & Year item preserved: _____

Running tally: _____

Amount put up: _____

Amount left over, or date ran out: _____

Comments: _____

_____

_____

Notes for next year: _____

Item Preserved: _____

Recipe or method used: _____

_____

_____

_____

_____

_____

_____

_____

_____

_____

_____

_____

_____

_____

_____

_____

_____

_____

_____

_____

_____

Month & Year item preserved: _____

Running tally: _____

Amount put up: _____

Amount left over, or date ran out: _____

Comments: _____

_____

Notes for next year: _____

_____

Pizza leather: Blend stewed tomatoes and tomato paste to baby food consistency; pour on drying tray, sprinkle with Italian seasonings and dehydrate.

Month & Year item preserved: _____

Running tally: _____

Amount put up: _____

Amount left over, or date ran out: _____

Comments: _____
_____
_____

Notes for next year: _____

Month & Year item preserved: _____

Running tally: _____

Amount put up: _____

Amount left over, or date ran out: _____

Comments: _____
_____
_____

Notes for next year: _____

Month & Year item preserved: _____

Running tally: _____

Amount put up: _____

Amount left over, or date ran out: _____

Comments: _____
_____
_____

Notes for next year: _____

Month & Year item preserved: _____

Running tally: _____

Amount put up: _____

Amount left over, or date ran out: _____

Comments: _____
_____
_____

Notes for next year: _____

Item Preserved: _____

Recipe or method used: ————————————

————————————————————————

————————————————————————

————————————————————————

————————————————————————

————————————————————————

————————————————————————

————————————————————————

————————————————————————

————————————————————————

————————————————————————

————————————————————————

————————————————————————

————————————————————————

————————————————————————

————————————————————————

————————————————————————

————————————————————————

————————————————————————

————————————————————————

————————————————————————

————————————————————————

Month &Year item preserved: ————————————

Running tally: ————————————————————

Amount put up: ————————————————————

Amount left over, or date ran out: —————————

Comments: —————————————————————

————————————————————————

Notes for next year: ————————————————

"The best preparation for tomorrow is to do today's work superbly well."
Sir William Osler

Month & Year item preserved: _____

Running tally: _____

Amount put up: _____

Amount left over, or date ran out: _____

Comments: _____

_____

_____

Notes for next year: _____

Month & Year item preserved: _____

Running tally: _____

Amount put up: _____

Amount left over, or date ran out: _____

Comments: _____

_____

_____

Notes for next year: _____

Month & Year item preserved: _____

Running tally: _____

Amount put up: _____

Amount left over, or date ran out: _____

Comments: _____

_____

_____

Notes for next year: _____

Month & Year item preserved: _____

Running tally: _____

Amount put up: _____

Amount left over, or date ran out: _____

Comments: _____

_____

_____

Notes for next year: _____

Item Preserved: _____

Recipe or method used: _____

_____

_____

_____

_____

_____

_____

_____

_____

_____

_____

_____

_____

_____

_____

_____

_____

_____

_____

_____

_____

_____

Month &Year item preserved: _____

Running tally: _____

Amount put up: _____

Amount left over, or date ran out: _____

Comments: _____

_____

_____

Notes for next year: _____

When freezing food in containers, first cover the food with crumpled up plastic wrap, then cover, to prevent freezer burn.

Month &Year item preserved: _____

Running tally: _____

Amount put up: _____

Amount left over, or date ran out: _____

Comments: _____
_____
_____

Notes for next year: _____

Month &Year item preserved: _____

Running tally: _____

Amount put up: _____

Amount left over, or date ran out: _____

Comments: _____
_____
_____

Notes for next year: _____

Month &Year item preserved: _____

Running tally: _____

Amount put up: _____

Amount left over, or date ran out: _____

Comments: _____
_____
_____

Notes for next year: _____

Month &Year item preserved: _____

Running tally: _____

Amount put up: _____

Amount left over, or date ran out: _____

Comments: _____
_____
_____

Notes for next year: _____

Item Preserved: —————————————————————

Recipe or method used: ————————————————

——————————————————————————————
——————————————————————————————
——————————————————————————————
——————————————————————————————
——————————————————————————————
——————————————————————————————
——————————————————————————————
——————————————————————————————
——————————————————————————————
——————————————————————————————
——————————————————————————————
——————————————————————————————
——————————————————————————————
——————————————————————————————
——————————————————————————————
——————————————————————————————
——————————————————————————————
——————————————————————————————
——————————————————————————————
——————————————————————————————
——————————————————————————————
——————————————————————————————

Month &Year item preserved: ————————————
Running tally: ——————————————————————
Amount put up: —————————————————————
Amount left over, or date ran out: ———————————
Comments: ——————————————————————————
——————————————————————————————
——————————————————————————————

Notes for next year: ————————————————————
——————————————————————————————

Before dehydrating bananas, dip in lemon juice
to enhance color and take away some of the sweetness.

Month & Year item preserved: _____

Running tally: _____

Amount put up: _____

Amount left over, or date ran out: _____

Comments: _____

_____

_____

Notes for next year: _____

Month & Year item preserved: _____

Running tally: _____

Amount put up: _____

Amount left over, or date ran out: _____

Comments: _____

_____

_____

Notes for next year: _____

Month & Year item preserved: _____

Running tally: _____

Amount put up: _____

Amount left over, or date ran out: _____

Comments: _____

_____

_____

Notes for next year: _____

Month & Year item preserved: _____

Running tally: _____

Amount put up: _____

Amount left over, or date ran out: _____

Comments: _____

_____

_____

Notes for next year: _____

Item Preserved: _____

Recipe or method used: _____

_____
_____
_____
_____
_____
_____
_____
_____
_____
_____
_____
_____
_____
_____
_____
_____
_____
_____
_____
_____
_____

Month & Year item preserved: _____
Running tally: _____
Amount put up: _____
Amount left over, or date ran out: _____
Comments: _____
_____
_____

Notes for next year: _____
_____

Baby socks are perfect spice bags!
Put spices in, tie and add to pickles.

Month &Year item preserved: _____

Running tally: _____

Amount put up: _____

Amount left over, or date ran out: _____

Comments: _____

_____

Notes for next year: _____

Month &Year item preserved: _____

Running tally: _____

Amount put up: _____

Amount left over, or date ran out: _____

Comments: _____

_____

Notes for next year: _____

Month &Year item preserved: _____

Running tally: _____

Amount put up: _____

Amount left over, or date ran out: _____

Comments: _____

_____

Notes for next year: _____

Month &Year item preserved: _____

Running tally: _____

Amount put up: _____

Amount left over, or date ran out: _____

Comments: _____

_____

Notes for next year: _____

Item Preserved: _____

Recipe or method used: _____

_____

_____

_____

_____

_____

_____

_____

_____

_____

_____

_____

_____

_____

_____

_____

_____

_____

_____

_____

_____

_____

_____

Month & Year item preserved: _____

Running tally: _____

Amount put up: _____

Amount left over, or date ran out: _____

Comments: _____

_____

Notes for next year: _____

_____

"The highest reward for a person's toil is not what they get for it, but what they become by it." John Ruskin

Month &Year item preserved: _____

Running tally: _____

Amount put up: _____

Amount left over, or date ran out: _____

Comments: _____

_____

_____

Notes for next year: _____

_____

Month &Year item preserved: _____

Running tally: _____

Amount put up: _____

Amount left over, or date ran out: _____

Comments: _____

_____

_____

Notes for next year: _____

_____

Month &Year item preserved: _____

Running tally: _____

Amount put up: _____

Amount left over, or date ran out: _____

Comments: _____

_____

_____

Notes for next year: _____

_____

Month &Year item preserved: _____

Running tally: _____

Amount put up: _____

Amount left over, or date ran out: _____

Comments: _____

_____

_____

Notes for next year: _____

_____

Item Preserved: _____

Recipe or method used: _____

_____

_____

_____

_____

_____

_____

_____

_____

_____

_____

_____

_____

_____

_____

_____

_____

_____

_____

_____

_____

_____

Month & Year item preserved: _____

Running tally: _____

Amount put up: _____

Amount left over, or date ran out: _____

Comments: _____

_____

_____

Notes for next year: _____

_____

To prevent a greasy rim on your jar when canning fish, keep the ring on
the jar. Pack fish, remove ring, wipe rim and put new lid and ring on.

Month &Year item preserved: _____

Running tally: _____

Amount put up: _____

Amount left over, or date ran out: _____

Comments: _____

_____

_____

Notes for next year: _____

_____

Month &Year item preserved: _____

Running tally: _____

Amount put up: _____

Amount left over, or date ran out: _____

Comments: _____

_____

_____

Notes for next year: _____

_____

Month &Year item preserved: _____

Running tally: _____

Amount put up: _____

Amount left over, or date ran out: _____

Comments: _____

_____

_____

Notes for next year: _____

_____

Month &Year item preserved: _____

Running tally: _____

Amount put up: _____

Amount left over, or date ran out: _____

Comments: _____

_____

_____

Notes for next year: _____

_____

*Item Preserved:*_____

Recipe or method used: _____

_____
_____
_____
_____
_____
_____
_____
_____
_____
_____
_____
_____
_____
_____
_____
_____
_____
_____
_____
_____
_____
_____

Month & Year item preserved: _____
Running tally: _____
Amount put up: _____
Amount left over, or date ran out: _____
Comments: _____
_____
_____

Notes for next year: _____
_____

"And the canning went on; early apples from our trees - magnificent prunes, petite prunes and red plums, whole and in conserve, damsons for jam ... "
James Beard, Delights & Predudices

Month &Year item preserved: _____

Running tally: _____

Amount put up: _____

Amount left over, or date ran out: _____

Comments: _____

_____

_____

Notes for next year: _____

_____

Month &Year item preserved: _____

Running tally: _____

Amount put up: _____

Amount left over, or date ran out: _____

Comments: _____

_____

_____

Notes for next year: _____

_____

Month &Year item preserved: _____

Running tally: _____

Amount put up: _____

Amount left over, or date ran out: _____

Comments: _____

_____

_____

Notes for next year: _____

_____

Month &Year item preserved: _____

Running tally: _____

Amount put up: _____

Amount left over, or date ran out: _____

Comments: _____

_____

_____

Notes for next year: _____

_____

Item Preserved: _____

Recipe or method used: _____

_____

_____

_____

_____

_____

_____

_____

_____

_____

_____

_____

_____

_____

_____

_____

_____

_____

_____

_____

_____

_____

_____

Month & Year item preserved: _____

Running tally: _____

Amount put up: _____

Amount left over, or date ran out: _____

Comments: _____

_____

_____

Notes for next year: _____

Before you U-pick, remember to call ahead, bring containers, wear "grubbies" and sturdy shoes and leave pets at home. Enjoy!

Month &Year item preserved: _____

Running tally: _____

Amount put up: _____

Amount left over, or date ran out: _____

Comments: _____

_____

_____

Notes for next year: _____

_____

Month &Year item preserved: _____

Running tally: _____

Amount put up: _____

Amount left over, or date ran out: _____

Comments: _____

_____

_____

Notes for next year: _____

_____

Month &Year item preserved: _____

Running tally: _____

Amount put up: _____

Amount left over, or date ran out: _____

Comments: _____

_____

_____

Notes for next year: _____

_____

Month &Year item preserved: _____

Running tally: _____

Amount put up: _____

Amount left over, or date ran out: _____

Comments: _____

_____

_____

Notes for next year: _____

_____

Item Preserved: _____

Recipe or method used: _____

_____

_____

_____

_____

_____

_____

_____

_____

_____

_____

_____

_____

_____

_____

_____

_____

_____

_____

_____

_____

_____

_____

Month & Year item preserved: _____

Running tally: _____

Amount put up: _____

Amount left over, or date ran out: _____

Comments: _____

_____

Notes for next year: _____

"What moistens the lips, what brightens the eye,
What calls back the past, like rich pumpkin pie?"
Old Jingle

80

Month & Year item preserved: _____

Running tally: _____

Amount put up: _____

Amount left over, or date ran out: _____

Comments: _____

_____

_____

Notes for next year: _____

_____

Month & Year item preserved: _____

Running tally: _____

Amount put up: _____

Amount left over, or date ran out: _____

Comments: _____

_____

_____

Notes for next year: _____

_____

Month & Year item preserved: _____

Running tally: _____

Amount put up: _____

Amount left over, or date ran out: _____

Comments: _____

_____

_____

Notes for next year: _____

_____

Month & Year item preserved: _____

Running tally: _____

Amount put up: _____

Amount left over, or date ran out: _____

Comments: _____

_____

_____

Notes for next year: _____

_____

Item Preserved: _____

Recipe or method used: _____

_____

_____

_____

_____

_____

_____

_____

_____

_____

_____

_____

_____

_____

_____

_____

_____

_____

_____

_____

Month &Year item preserved: _____

Running tally: _____

Amount put up: _____

Amount left over, or date ran out: _____

Comments: _____

_____

Notes for next year: _____

Select corn that has bright-green snug husks and dark-brown silks (a sign of full kernals). 3 ears of fresh corn = 1 cup kernals.

Month &Year item preserved: _____

Running tally: _____

Amount put up: _____

Amount left over, or date ran out: _____

Comments: _____

_____

_____

Notes for next year: _____

Month &Year item preserved: _____

Running tally: _____

Amount put up: _____

Amount left over, or date ran out: _____

Comments: _____

_____

_____

Notes for next year: _____

Month &Year item preserved: _____

Running tally: _____

Amount put up: _____

Amount left over, or date ran out: _____

Comments: _____

_____

_____

Notes for next year: _____

Month &Year item preserved: _____

Running tally: _____

Amount put up: _____

Amount left over, or date ran out: _____

Comments: _____

_____

_____

Notes for next year: _____

_____

Yield Conversions

*W*e annually press apples for juice from free apples we are fortunate to receive. One year no free apples were available. Should we buy apples? How many? Estimates varied, but 10 pounds of apples per gallon seemed the average guess. But we found, after a day's work and 700 pounds of apples that we had a disappointing 36 gallons of delicious but expensive apple juice. Thus my hard-won conversion was 19 1/2 pounds of apples = 1 gallon of juice.

This page is also useful for planting a garden. How many tomato plants do you need for 50 quarts? There are some standard references, see the next page, but you will want to note your experiences.

Produce	*Yield*	*Note*

Conserves differ from marmalades in that several fruits are often combined and nuts are usually added. Add nuts after cooking to avoid toughening.

Yield Conversions

Raw Produce	Approximate Weight	Amount Yielded
Fruits:		
Apples	48 pound bushel	16-19 quarts
Applesauce	48 pound bushel	14-19 quarts
Apricots	50 pound bushel	20-25 quarts
Berries (whole)	36 pound crate	18-24 quarts
Cherries	25 pound lug	8-12 quarts
Grapes (whole)	26 pound lug	12-14 quarts
Nectarines	48 pound bushel	16-24 quarts
Peaches (halved/sliced)	48 pound bushel	16-24 quarts
Pears (halved)	50 pound bushel	16-25 quarts
Plums (halved/whole)	56 pound bushel	22-36 quarts
Rhubarb	28 pound lug	14-28 quarts
Vegetables:		
Asparagus	31 pound crate	7-12 quarts
Beans, lima, shelled	32 pound bushel	6-10 quarts
Beans, snap green/wax	30 pound bushel	12-20 quarts
Beets, (sliced/cubed/ whole, w/o tops)	52 pound bushel	15-20 quarts
Carrots, (sliced, cubed, whole, w/o tops)	50 pound bushel	17-25 quarts
Corn, cream style	35 pound bushel (in husk)	12-20 quarts
Corn, whole kernel	35 pound bushel (in husk)	6-11 quarts
Peas, green or English, (in pod)	30 pound bushel	4-6 quarts
Peppers, hot or sweet	25 pound bushel	20-30 pints
Potatoes, sweet	50 pound bushel·	17-25 quarts
Potatoes, white (cubed, whole)	50 pound bag	8-12 quarts
Pumpkin, winter squash, (cubed)	50 pound bushel	4-9 quarts
Spinach, other greens	18 pound bushel	4-9 quarts
Herbs:		
Herbs, general	8 ounces, fresh	1 ounce, dried

Preserved Gift Log

*O*ne of the most rewarding aspects of food preserving is having unique, delicious and already prepared homemade gifts on hand throughout the year. Chutneys, dilly beans, flavored vinegars, jams, mustards, pickles, etc. are special gifts only you can give. To keep track of what you've given to the special people in your life each year and how it was received, just write it in on this handy journal log.

Gift	Name	Date	Notes

"That is your poem - too tenuous for a book;
You are a very gentle, perfect cook." *Walter Lowenfels*

Preserved Gift Log

Gift	Name	Date	Notes

Ball Consumer Affairs Dept., Alltrista Corp., 1-800-428-8150
PO Box 2729, Muncie, IN 47302 Free "Consumer Newsline" magazine or "Home Canners Catalog"

Kerr Consumer Products, 1-800-344-5377
PO Box 1179, Jackson, TN 38302-1179 Free newsletter available

Kraft General Foods, 250 North St., White Plains, NY 10625 1-800-437-3284
(Sure-Jel/Sure-Jel Light/Certo/Slim-Set/MCP/Ever Fresh)

Heinz Vinegar, 1062 Progress St., Pittsburg, PA 15212 412-237-5740

ReaLemon by Borden, Borden Consumer Response, 1-800-426-7336
180 Ed. Broad St., Columbus, OH 43215

FDA Seafood Hotline, 200 C St SW, Washington, DC 20204 1-800-FDA-4010

USDA Meat and Poultry Hotline, 1-800-535-4555
USDA-FSIS, 14th & Independence SW, Rm 2925, Washington, DC 20250

Extension Agency,* _____

* Check your phonebook for your county number or call any nearby University and they can provide your local number.

Extension is an off-campus educational arm from the Land-Grant Universities in each state. They offer educational programs and information related to: agriculture, foods and nutrition, food preservation, forestry, horticulture, livestock, 4-H and youth development.

Other Reference Numbers:

_____

_____

_____

_____

_____

_____

_____

_____

_____

_____

_____

Canning & Preservation Sources

Ball Blue Book, Box 2005, Muncie, IN 47302
1-800-428-8150
Guide to home canning & freezing, lists jars, lids available in retail stores.

Bernardin of Canada, Ltd., 120 The East Mall, Toronto, Ontario, M8Z 5V5
416-239-4424   Home canning guide, with new procedures & recipes.

Berry-Hill Ltd., 75 Burwell Rd., St Thomas, Ontario N5P 3R5
Free catalog features canning equipment, supplies, cider press & garden.

Dacus, Inc., P.O. Box 2067, Tupelo, MS. 38803-2067 1-800-647-8170
Free pamphlet of "Mrs Wages" products for home canning, pickles, jams, etc.

Farmer Seed & Nursery Co., 818 NW 4th St, Faribault, MN 55021
507-334-1623
Free catalog features canning equipment, accessories, supplies, seeds & plants.

Gardener's Kitchen, PO Box 322, Monument Beach, MA. 02553
Free list of products, includes canning rings & lids.

Glashaus/Weck Home Canning, 415 W Golf Rd., Ste. 13, Arlington Heights, IL
60005   847-640-6910
Free catalog features canning supplies & equipment.

Gurney Seed & Nursery Co., 110 Capitol St., Yankton, SD 57079
605-665-1930
Free catalog features canning equipment, supplies & seeds.

Home Canning Supply & Specialties Catalog, P.O. Box 1158, Ramona, CA.
92065 Free catalog features food preserving supplies, crocks, apple presses, etc.

Mellinger's Inc., 2328 W. South Range Rd., North Lima, OH 44452
216-549-9861   Free catalog features canning equipment & supplies.

Olshen's Bottle Supply Co., 1204 SE Water Ave., Portland, OR 97214
1-800-259-4292 Free brochure of plastic, glass and metal containers & lids.

Freezing Herbs

*I*f you want the taste of fresh herbs all year long, consider freezing them. Many herbs can be frozen with results close to fresh herbs. Simply wash them, then blanch for a few seconds. Just hold them in the water by their stems, then remove when their color brightens. Or microwave them briefly, just until color brightens. Blot herbs dry with a paper towel and cool. Wrap in freezer strength plastic wrap and place in freezer bags, freeze. When herbs thaw, they are limp and not recommended as a garnish but excellent for cooking.

Herbs that freeze well:	Chives	Mint family
Angelica	Comfrey	Parsley family
Anise hyssop	Coriander	Plantain
Basil, sweet	Dandilion, common	Savory
Blackberry	Dill	Sorrel
Burnet, salad	Fennel, sweet	Thyme
Chervil	Lamb's quarters	
_____	_____	_____
_____	_____	_____
_____	_____	_____

"Medea gather'd the enchanted herbs. That did renew old Aeson".
The Merchant of Venice

Storage of Preserved Foods

Canned: Once lids are sealed onto jars, remove screw bands and wash jar to remove any food. Label and date jars. Store in a cool, dark and dry place. Do not store jars above 95°F (35°C), or near hot pipes, furnaces or sunlight. (They could lose vitamin C, quality and even spoil under those conditions.) Properly canned and stored foods will keep indefinately, but after a year some chemical changes do occur and the quality of taste and appearance diminshes.

Frozen: Follow these steps for quality fruits, vegetables and herbs that can last up to a year in the freezer.

1. Start with food in quality condition. **2.** Properly blanch, if necessary. **3.** Properly package with freezer bags or rigid freezer containers. Leave no air pockets if possible. **4.** Freeze rapidly and store at 0°F (-18°C), or lower. **5.** Use within a reasonable time and use the oldest products first. Keep an inventory.

Dried: Dried foods should be stored in airtight, sterilized containers and in a cool, dark place, below 60°F (16°C). If dried foods are frozen at 34°F (1°C), or cooler, they can easily last over a year.

*F*reezer failure can panic anybody and is a possibility whether it's from mechanical problems, human error or power failure.

First and foremost do not open your freezer. This lets warm air in and cold air out. In a well filled freezer, food will not thaw for 15-20 hours, less if not full. Try to determine the reason for failure and if necessary call a repairman. If you anticipate your food thawing before your freezer is back in operation, you have several options.

Option 1: Dry ice may be placed (with gloves on), inside the freezer. Lay dry ice on top of heavy cardboard which is placed on the food. In addition, blankets can provide extra insulation when put on top of the freezer. A 50 pound cake of dry ice is enough to protect solidly frozen food in a 20 cubic freezer for 36 hours. Dry ice often leaves an odor, but it is harmless to food.

Option 2: Snow and ice can be utilized for temporary storage too. Take a garbage can and line with a garbage bag. Put frozen food into lined can, tie bag, and put the lid on tightly. Bury the can in snow and it should stay frozen for 4 or 5 days.

Option 3: Food may be moved to a working freezer or rent locker freezer space.

Once your freezer is working again, check to see if any food has thawed. Thawed food may be refrozen if it has been thawed no longer than two days, kept at a temperature no higher than 45 °F (7°C), and does not show signs of spoilage. Partially thawed food may be safely refrozen if it still contains ice crystals. It's a good idea to mark your refrozen foods so they will be used first.

For Emergency Freezer Service Contact:

_____

_____

_____

_____

Notes: _____

_____

_____

For the freshest frozen fish,
put the fish into a milk carton with water.
The water keeps the fish fresh and the cartons are easy to stack in the freezer.

Canning Equipment

*7*here are two methods of canning: boiling water (water bath) canning and pressure canning. Here is some important information regarding these two types of canning and their equipment.

Boiling water canning is used for high acids foods such as fruits and most people prefer this method. The boiling water canners are made of aluminum or porcelain-covered steel. They should have a removable perforated rack for jars to rest on. The canner must be deep enough so that at least 1" of briskly boiling water will be over the tops of jars during processing. A flat bottom works best on an electric range, but flat or ridged bottoms will work with gas burners. The canner should be no more than 4" wider in diameter than the element to ensure uniform processing of all jars.

Pressure canners are used to can low acid foods (meat, vegetables, poultry and fish). Only pressure canners can reach temperatures high enough (240°F/116°C) to kill harmful bacteria which grow in these foods. Pressure canners should have an accurate dial gauge or weighted gauge to indicate pressure. They usually have a gasket to keep the steam from leaking out around the cover. A petcock, safety valve, or weight is used to control the escape of the air or steam. The canner should also have a rack to hold the jars off the bottom of the canner.

The difference between weighted and dial gauge canners is one of personal preference. Here are some thoughts to consider:

Dial Gauge Advantages:

1. Can be very useful in high-altitudes. Can adjust to as little as 1/2 lb. pressure
2. Quieter than a weighted gauge

Disadvantages:

1. Gauge must be tested yearly for accuracy
2. Needs to be watched to maintain pressure and takes some getting used to
3. More parts

Weighted Gauge Advantages:

1. Simple to operate
2. Fewer parts to break
3. Always accurate, (unless weight is damaged)
4. Do not have to watch constantly, since the weight can be heard jiggling, which indicates correct pressure
5. Good for people who prefer listening for, as opposed to watching a gauge

Disadvantages:

1. Sound may be annoying
2. Cannot adjust for high-altitudes, other than in 5 lb. increments of weights

Canning Equipment Care

Follow these steps for pressure canner care:

1. Have your dial gauge canner checked yearly for accuracy (your Extension Service should be able to help you with this).
2. See that the petcock and safety valve are not blocked and use a pipe cleaner to clean them frequently.
3. If a gasket becomes loose, cracked or brittle it should be replaced.
4. Wash and dry canner after each use.

Canning jar care:

Canning jars are available in 1/2 pint, pint, 1 1/2 pint, quart and 1/2 gallon sizes in regular and wide mouth tops. Half gallon jars may only be used to can very acid fruit juices. Also available for canning are the 8 and12 ounce decorator jelly jars. With careful use and handling jars may be used for many years requiring only new lids each time. Most commercial pint and quart mayonnaise type jars may be used in a boiling water canner. These jars should not be used in a pressure canner. The chances of a non-standard jar breaking or not sealing are greater than for standard canning jars. Before using a commercial jar, check carefully for the following:

1. Even thickness of glass in sides, bottom and top.
2. No evidence of stress, bubbles, or uneven places in the glass.
3. Proper depth of jar neck so band will screw all the way down.
4. Continuous threads to hold the screw band firmly.
5. Standard shape and size (pint and quart).

*Before every use, wash empty jars in hot soapy water and rinse well.
Scale or hard-water films are easily removed by soaking jars several hours
in a solution of 1 cup of vinegar per gallon of water.*

Lids and Screwbands:

The common self-sealing lid consists of a flat metal disc held in place by a metal screwband during processing. When jars are processed, the lid gasket softens and flows slightly to cover the jar sealing surface, yet allows air to escape from the jar. The gasket then forms an airtight seal as the jar cools. Examine all metal lids carefully. Do not use old, dented, or deformed lids, or lids with gaps or other defects in the sealing compound. Do not retighten lids after processing. As jars cool, the contents contract, pulling the self-sealing lid firmly against the jar to form a vacuum.

Screwbands are not needed on stored jars; remove after jars have cooled. After removing, wash and dry the bands; store in a dry area. With care, the bands may be reused many times. If left on stored jars, they become difficult to remove, often rust and may not be reusable.

"Have a Victory Garden -
Eat what you can, and can what you can't eat."
Victory Gardening Booklet

The *Preserver's Journal* and other cooking and food hobby books
published by Culinary Arts Ltd., may be found in
book, cooking, gift, and specialty stores.
If you have difficulty finding a title in your area, please contact
the publisher. Publishers's free catalog available upon request.
(Outside the U.S. add $2.00 for postage, refundable with order.)

Culinary Arts Ltd.
Publishers of Unique Specialty Books
P.O. Box 2157, Lake Oswego, Oregon 97035
Phone: 503-639-4549   Fax: 503-620-4933

Current titles from Culinary Arts Ltd.:

Classic Liqueurs: The Art of Making & Cooking with Liqueurs
Cheryl Long & Heather Kibbey

Easy Microwave Preserving: The Shortcut Way to Preserve
Cynthia Fischborn & Cheryl Long

Gourmet Mustards: How to Make & Cook with Them
Helene Sawyer

Gourmet Vinegars: How to Make & Cook with Them
Marsha Peters Johnson

Lamb Country Cooking: Lamb with All the Trimmings
Jill Stanford Warren

Preserver's Journal: Putting Down What You Put Up
Diane Dunas

***The Best of Scanfest: An Authentic Treasury of Recipes & Proverbs
from Denmark, Finland, Iceland, Norway & Sweden***
Cheryl Long, Editor